CU00406305

U.S. DEPARTMENT OF JUSTICE
FEDERAL BUREAU OF INVESTIGATION
WASHINGTON, D.C. 20535-0001
BANK CRIME STATISTICS (BCS)
FEDERALLY INSURED FINANCIAL INSTITUTIONS
January 1, 2015 - December 31, 2015

I. VIOLATIONS OF THE FEDERAL BANK ROBBERY AND INCIDENTAL CRIMES STATUTE, TITLE 18, UNITED STATES CODE, SECTION 2113

Violations by Type of Institution

	Robberies	Burglaries	Larcenies
Commercial Banks	3,543	45	6
Mutual Savings Banks	17	1	0
Savings and Loan Associations	102	0	0
Credit Unions	340	6	1
Armored Carrier Companies	28	1	1
Totals:	4,030	53	8

Grand Total - All Violations: 4,091

Number, Race, and Sex of Perpetrators

The number of persons known to be involved in the 4,091 robberies, burglaries, and larcenies was 4,817. The following table shows a breakdown of the 4,817 persons by race and sex. In a small number of cases the use of full disguise makes determination of race and sex impossible.

	White	Black	Hispanic	Other	Unknown
Male	1781	2026	277	85	219
Female	168	155	24	3	9

Unknown Race/Sex: 70

Investigation to date has resulted in the identification of 2,731 (57 percent) of the 4,817 persons known to be involved. Of these 2,731 identified persons, 1,035 (38 percent) were determined to be users of narcotics, and 550 (20 percent) were found to have been previously convicted in either federal or state court for bank robbery, bank burglary, or bank larceny.

Occurrences by Day of Week and Time of Day

Monday	–	672	6-9 a.m.	–	120
Tuesday	–	710	9-11 a.m.	–	1,042
Wednesday	–	672	11 a.m.-1 p.m.	–	933
Thursday	–	652	1-3 p.m.	–	890
Friday	–	789	3-6 p.m.	–	990
Saturday	–	356	6 p.m.-6 a.m.	–	114
Sunday	–	51	Not Determined	–	2
Not Determined	–	188			
Total:		**4,090**	**Total:**		**4,091**

Institution/Community Characteristics

Type of Financial Institution Office

Main Office	78
Branch Office	3,926
Store	66
Remote Facility/Other	21
Total:	**4,091**

Location of Financial Institution Office

Commercial District	2,699
Shopping Center	999
Residential	244
Other Location	149
Total:	**4,091**

Community Type

Metropolitan	1,940
Suburban	668
Small City/Town	1,408
Rural	75
Total:	**4,091**

Institutional Areas Involved

Counter	3,920	Night Depository	1
Vault/Safe	146	Automatic Teller Machine	44
Safe Deposit Area	11	Courier/Messenger	1
Office Area	116	Armored Vehicle	2
Drive-In/Walk-Up	29	Other	52

Modus Operandi Used

Demand note Used	2,416
Firearm Used[1]	877
Handgun	848
Other Firearm	36
Other Weapon Used[2]	25
Weapon Threatened[3]	1,762
Explosive Device Used or Threatened	108
Oral Demand	2,146
Vault or Safe Theft	11
Depository Trap Device	0
Till Theft	44
Takeover	186

---

[1] "Handgun" and "Other Firearm" added together may not coincide with "Firearm Used" since, in some cases, both handguns and other firearms are used during the same crime.

[2] "Other Weapon Used" includes knives, other cutting instruments, hypodermic needles, clubs, etc.

[3] "Weapon Threatened" includes those cases where a weapon was threatened or implied either orally or in a demand note but not actually observed.

Injuries, Deaths, and Hostages Taken

Acts of violence were committed during 137 (3 percent) of the 4,091 robberies, burglaries, and larcenies that occurred during this timeframe. These acts included 37 instances involving the discharge of firearms, one instance involving explosives, and 85 instances involving assaults. (One or more acts of violence may occur during an incident.) These acts of violence resulted in 57 injuries, 9 deaths, and 56 persons taken hostage.

Injuries

Customer	10
Employee	35
Employee Family	0
Perpetrator	9
Law Officer	0
Guard	1
Other	2
Total:	**57**

Number of violations in which injuries occurred: 44

Deaths

Customer	0
Employee	0
Employee Family	0
Perpetrator	8
Law Officer	0
Guard	0
Other	1
Total:	**9**

Number of violations in which deaths occurred: 9

Hostages Taken

Customer	12
Employee	40
Employee Family	1
Law Officer	0
Guard	0
Other	3
Total:	**56**

Number of violations in which hostages were taken: 20

II. BANK EXTORTION VIOLATIONS WHICH WERE INVESTIGATED UNDER THE FEDERAL BANKROBBERY AND INCIDENTAL CRIMES STATUTE, TITLE 18, UNITED STATES CODE, SECTION 2113
January 1, 2015 - December 31, 2015

Violations by Type of Institution

Commercial Banks	3
Mutual Savings Banks	0
Savings and Loan Associations	0
Credit Unions	3
Armored Carrier Companies	0
Total:	**6**

Number, Race, and Sex of Perpetrators

The number of persons known to be involved in the six bank extortion incidents was eleven. In a number of cases the number and description of individuals involved is unknown due to nonobservance of the perpetrator by the victim(s) or the use of disguises. The following table shows a breakdown of the five known individuals involved by race and sex:

	White	Black	Hispanic	Other	Unknown
Male	7	1	1	0	1
Female	1	0	0	0	0

Unknown Race/Sex: 0

Occurrences by Day of Week and Time of Day

Monday	-	1	6-9 a.m.	-	3
Tuesday	-	2	9-11 a.m.	-	2
Wednesday	-	2	11 a.m.-1 p.m.	-	0
Thursday	-	1	1-3 p.m.	-	0
Friday	-	0	3-6 p.m.	-	1
Saturday	-	0	6 p.m.-6 a.m.	-	0
Sunday	-	0	Not Determined	-	0
Not Determined	-	0			
Total:		**6**	**Total:**		**6**

Institution/Community Characteristics

Type of Financial Institution Office

Main Office	2
Branch Office	4
Store	0
Remote Facility/Other	0
Total:	**6**

Location of Financial Institution Office

Commercial District	5
Shopping Center	0
Residential	1
Other Location	0
Total:	**6**

Community Type

Metropolitan	1
Suburban	2
Small City/Town	3
Rural	0
Total:	**6**

Modus Operandi Used

Demand note Used	2
Firearm Used[4]	5
Other Weapon Used	0
Weapon Threatened[5]	3
Explosive Device Used or Threatened	1
Telephone Call	0

Injuries, Deaths, and Hostages Taken

Acts of violence were committed during four of the six bank extortion incidents that occurred during this timeframe. No deaths occurred when the violent acts were committed. However, one person was injured and twelve persons were taken hostage during four of the bank extortion incidents.

Injuries

Customer	0
Employee	1
Employee Family	0
Perpetrator	0
Law Officer	0
Guard	0
Other	0
Total:	**1**

Number of violations in which injuries occurred: 1

---

[4] "Handgun" and "Other Firearm" added together may not coincide with "Firearm Used" since, in some cases, both handguns and other firearms are used during the same crime.
[5] "Weapon Threatened" includes those cases where a weapon was threatened or implied either orally or in a demand note but not actually observed.

Hostages Taken

Customer	0
Employee	4
Employee Family	8
Law Officer	0
Guard	0
Other	0
Total:	**12**

Number of violations in which hostages were taken: 4

III. BANK ROBBERY STATUE VIOLATIONS BY REGIONS, GEOGRAPHIC DIVISION, STATES, AND TERRITORIES
January 1, 2015 - December 31, 2015

	BANK ROBBERIES	BANK BURGLARIES	BANK LARCENIES	BANK EXTORTIONS
REGIONAL SUMMARY				
NORTHEAST	931	6	0	0
NORTH CENTRAL	815	6	4	1
SOUTH	1,242	22	3	4
WEST	1,038	19	1	1
TERRITORIES	4	0	0	0
Totals:	4,030	53	8	6
NORTHEAST	931	6	0	0
NEW ENGLAND	320	2	0	0
CONNECTICUT	103	1	0	0
MAINE	10	0	0	0
MASSACHUSETTS	147	1	0	0
NEW HAMPSHIRE	30	0	0	0
RHODE ISLAND	17	0	0	0
VERMONT	13	0	0	0
MIDDLE ATLANTIC	611	4	0	0
NEW JERSEY	108	2	0	0
NEW YORK	243	2	0	0
PENNSYLVANIA	260	0	0	0
NORTH CENTRAL	815	6	4	1
EAST NORTH CENTRAL	630	5	0	1
ILLINOIS	179	0	0	0
INDIANA	94	0	0	0
MICHIGAN	91	4	0	0
OHIO	152	0	0	1
WISCONSIN	114	1	0	0
WEST NORTH CENTRAL	185	1	4	0
IOWA	23	0	0	0
KANSAS	22	1	0	0
MINNESOTA	43	0	0	0
MISSOURI	76	0	1	0
NEBRASKA	14	0	3	0
NORTH DAKOTA	5	0	0	0
SOUTH DAKOTA	2	0	0	0

SOUTH	1,242	22	3	4
SOUTH ATLANTIC	807	10	2	0
DELAWARE	22	0	0	0
DISTRICT OF COLUMBIA	28	1	0	0
FLORIDA	240	4	0	0
GEORGIA	107	1	0	0
MARYLAND	138	0	0	0
NORTH CAROLINA	106	1	1	0
SOUTH CAROLINA	50	1	0	0
VIRGINIA	106	2	1	0
WEST VIRGINIA	10	0	0	0
EAST SOUTH CENTRAL	117	5	0	4
ALABAMA	27	1	0	0
KENTUCKY	37	1	0	0
MISSISSIPPI	14	3	0	0
TENNESSEE	39	0	0	4
WEST SOUTH CENTRAL	318	7	1	0
ARKANSAS	18	3	0	0
LOUISIANA	20	2	0	0
OKLAHOMA	17	0	1	0
TEXAS	263	2	0	0
WEST	1,038	19	1	1
MOUNTAIN	383	3	0	1
ARIZONA	126	2	0	0
COLORADO	89	0	0	0
IDAHO	9	0	0	0
MONTANA	0	1	0	0
NEVADA	63	0	0	0
NEW MEXICO	40	0	0	0
UTAH	55	0	0	1
WYOMING	1	0	0	0
PACIFIC	655	16	1	0
ALASKA	7	0	0	0
CALIFORNIA	473	12	0	0
HAWAII	13	0	0	0
OREGON	58	0	0	0
WASHINGTON	104	4	1	0
TERRITORIES	4	0	0	0
GUAM	0	0	0	0
PUETO RICO	4	0	0	0
VIRGIN ISLANDS	0	0	0	0
Totals:	4,030	53	8	6

IV. VIOLATIONS INVOLVING ARMORED CARRIERS INVESTIGATED UNDER THE HOBBS ACT TITLE 18, UNITED STATES CODE, SECTION 1951
January 1, 2015 - December 31, 2015

Armored Carrier Violations

Hobbs Act	26
Total:	**26**

Number, Race, and Sex of Perpetrators

The number of persons known to be involved in the 26 armored carrier incidents was 50. In a number of cases the number and description of individuals involved is unknown due to nonobservance of the perpetrator by the victim(s) or the use of disguises. The following table shows a breakdown of the 50 known individuals involved by race and sex:

	White	Black	Hispanic	Other	Unknown
Male	2	28	8	3	4
Female	0	0	1	0	1

Unknown Race/Sex: 3

Occurrences by Day of Week and Time of Day

Monday	-	4	6-9 a.m.	-	6
Tuesday	-	3	9-11 a.m.	-	4
Wednesday	-	2	11 a.m.-1 p.m.	-	7
Thursday	-	4	1-3 p.m.	-	4
Friday	-	9	3-6 p.m.	-	4
Saturday	-	2	6 p.m.-6 a.m.	-	1
Sunday	-	2	Not Determined	-	0
Not Determined	-	0			
Total:		**26**	**Total:**		**26**

Community Characteristics

Location

Commercial District	13
Shopping Center	9
Residential	2
Other Location	2
Total:	**26**

Community Type

Metropolitan	16
Suburban	1
Small City/Town	9
Rural	0
Total:	**26**

Modus Operandi Used

Firearm Used[6]	17
Handgun	17
Other Firearm	2
Other Weapon Used[7]	4
Weapon Threatened[8]	4
Explosive Device Used or Threatened	0
Oral Demand	11
Vault or Safe Theft	0

Injuries, Deaths, and Hostages Taken

Acts of violence were committed during 15 of the 26 armored carrier incidents, which occurred during this timeframe. No hostages were taken when the violent acts were committed. These acts of violence resulted in 11 injuries and one death. (One or more acts of violence may occur during an incident.)

Injuries

Customer	0
Employee	0
Employee Family	0
Perpetrator	2
Law Officer	0
Guard	9
Other	0
Total:	**11**

Number of violations in which injuries occurred: 9

Deaths

Customer	0
Employee	1
Employee Family	0
Perpetrator	0
Law Officer	0
Guard	0
Other	0
Total:	**1**

Number of violations in which deaths occurred: 1

---

[6] "Handgun" and "Other Firearm" added together may not coincide with "Firearm Used" since, in some cases, both handguns and firearms are used during the same crime.

[7] "Other Weapon Used" includes knives, other cutting instruments, hypodermic needles, clubs, etc.

[8] "Weapon Threatened" includes those cases where a weapon was threatened or implied either orally or in a demand note but was not actually observed.

Any statistical information furnished in this booklet is
subject to change upon the investigation of bank robbery incidents,
which occurred during 2015.

The BCS provides a nationwide view of bank robbery crimes based on
statistics contributed by FBI field offices responding to bank robberies or
otherwise gathered when provided to the FBI from local and state law
enforcement.

Statistics recorded as of 3/23/2016, at FBI Headquarters.

NOTE: Not all Bank Robberies are reported to the FBI, and therefore BCS is
not a complete statistical compilation of all Bank Robberies that occur in
the United States.

U.S. DEPARTMENT OF JUSTICE
FEDERAL BUREAU OF INVESTIGATION
WASHINGTON, D.C. 20535-0001
BANK CRIME STATISTICS (BCS)
FEDERALLY INSURED FINANCIAL INSTITUTIONS
January 1, 2016 - December 31, 2016

I. VIOLATIONS OF THE FEDERAL BANK ROBBERY AND INCIDENTAL CRIMES STATUTE,
TITLE 18, UNITED STATES CODE, SECTION 2113

Violations by Type of Institution

	Robberies	Burglaries	Larcenies
Commercial Banks	3,733	48	0
Mutual Savings Banks	27	1	0
Savings and Loan Associations	65	0	0
Credit Unions	343	12	1
Armored Carrier Companies	17	4	0
Totals:	4,185	65	1

Grand Total - All Violations: 4,251

Number, Race, and Sex of Perpetrators

The number of persons known to be involved in the 4,251 robberies,
burglaries, and larcenies was 4,900. The following table shows a breakdown
of the 4,900 persons by race and sex. In a small number of cases, the use of
full disguise makes determination of race and sex impossible.

	White	Black	Hispanic	Asian	Other	Unknown
Male	1,797	2,164	252	14	49	253
Female	185	131	10	2	8	11

Unknown Race/Sex: 24

Investigation to date has resulted in the identification of 2,537 of the
4,900 persons known to be involved. Of these 2,537 identified persons,
40 percent were determined to be users of narcotics, and 27 percent were
found to have been previously convicted in either federal or state court for
bank robbery, bank burglary, or bank larceny.

Occurrences by Day of Week and Time of Day

Monday	-	728	6-9 a.m.	-	99
Tuesday	-	741	9-11 a.m.	-	1,004
Wednesday	-	758	11 a.m.-1 p.m.	-	961
Thursday	-	699	1-3 p.m.	-	800
Friday	-	913	3-6 p.m.	-	923
Saturday	-	361	6 p.m.-6 a.m.	-	455
Sunday	-	51	Not Determined	-	9
Not Determined	-	0			
Total:		4,251	Total:		4,251

Institution/Community Characteristics

Type of Financial Institution Office

Main Office	144
Branch Office	3,978
Store	112
Remote Facility/Other	17
Total:	**4,251**

Location of Financial Institution Office

Commercial District	2,725
Shopping Center	1,026
Residential	365
Other Location	135
Total:	**4,251**

Community Type

Metropolitan	1,997
Suburban	838
Small City/Town	1,297
Rural	110
Unknown	9
Total:	**4,251**

Institutional Areas Involved

Counter	4,054
Night Depository	3
Vault/Safe	147
Auto. Teller Machine	45
Safe Deposit Area	11
Courier/Messenger	1
Office Area	128
Armored Vehicle	5
Drive-In/Walk-Up	34
Other	31
Cash Kiosk	4

Security Devices Maintained By Victim Institutions

Alarm System	4,085
Surveillance Cameras	4,210
Bait Money	1,942
Guards	224
Currency Dye/Gas Packs	709
Electronic Tracking Devices	595
Bullet-Resistant Enclosures	610
Access-Controlled Entry-Way	56
Man Trap	36

Security Devices Used During Crimes

Alarm System Activated	3,669
Surveillance Cameras Activated	4,057
Bait Money Taken	900
Guards on Duty	177
Currency Dye/Gas Packs Taken	240
Electronic Tracking Devices Activated	292
Man Trap Activated	12
Access-Controlled Entry-Way	24

Security Devices Functioned

Alarm System Functioned	3,519
Surveillance Cameras Functioned	3,887
Electronic Tracking Devices Functioned	266

Modus Operandi Used

Demand Note Used	2,267
Firearm Used	590
Handgun[1]	965
Other Firearm	36
Other Weapon Used[2]	26
Weapon Threatened[3]	2,361
Explosive Device Used or Threatened	110
Oral Demand	1,958
Vault or Safe Theft	25
Depository Trap Device	11
Till Theft	48
Takeover	285

---

[1] 'Handgun' and 'Other Firearm' added together may not coincide with 'Firearm Used' since, in some cases, both handguns and other firearms are used in the same crime.

[2] 'Other Weapon Used' includes knives, other cutting instruments, clubs, etc.

[3] 'Weapon Threatened' includes those cases where a weapon was threatened or implied either orally or in a demand note but not actually observed.

Injuries, Deaths, and Hostages Taken

Acts of violence were committed during 146 of the 4,251 robberies, burglaries, and larcenies that occurred during this time frame. These acts included 43 instances involving the discharge of firearms, 72 instances involving assaults, and 31 instances involving a hostage taken.
(One or more acts of violence may occur during an incident.)
These acts of violence resulted in 43 injuries, 8 deaths, and 59 persons taken hostage.

Injuries

Customer	9
Employee	23
Employee Family	0
Perpetrator	8
Law Officer	0
Guard	2
Other	1
Total:	**43**

Number of violations in which injuries occurred: 37

Deaths

Customer	0
Employee	1
Employee Family	0
Perpetrator	7
Law Officer	0
Guard	0
Other	0
Total:	**8**

Number of violations in which deaths occurred: 7

Hostages Taken

Customer	21
Employee	32
Employee Family	0
Law Officer	1
Guard	3
Other	2
Total:	**59**

Number of violations in which hostages were taken: 31

II. BANK EXTORTION VIOLATIONS WHICH WERE INVESTIGATED UNDER THE FEDERAL BANK ROBBERY AND INCIDENTAL CRIMES STATUTE, TITLE 18, UNITED STATES CODE, SECTION 2113
January 1, 2016 - December 31, 2016

Violations by Type of Institution

Commercial Banks	2
Mutual Savings Banks	0
Savings and Loan Associations	0
Credit Unions	1
Armored Carrier Companies	0
Total:	**3**

Number, Race, and Sex of Perpetrators

The number of persons known to be involved in the three bank extortion violations was three. In a number of cases the number and description of individuals involved is unknown due to nonobservance of the perpetrators by the victim(s) or the use of disguises. The following table shows a breakdown of the three known individuals involved by race and sex:

	White	Black	Hispanic	Asian	Other	Unknown
Male	3	0	0	0	0	0
Female	0	0	0	0	0	0

Occurrences by Day of Week and Time of Day

Monday	-	0	6-9 a.m.	-	2
Tuesday	-	1	9-11 a.m.	-	0
Wednesday	-	0	11 a.m.-1 p.m.	-	0
Thursday	-	1	1-3 p.m.	-	0
Friday	-	0	3-6 p.m.	-	1
Saturday	-	1	6 p.m.-6 a.m.	-	0
Sunday	-	0	Not Determined	-	0
Not Determined	-	0			
Total:		**3**	**Total:**		**3**

Institution/Community Characteristics

Type of Financial Institution Office

Main Office	0
Branch Office	3
Store	0
Remote Facility/Other	0
Total:	**3**

Location of Financial Institution Office

Commercial District	2
Shopping Center	1
Residential	0
Other Location	0
Total:	**3**

Community Type

Metropolitan	1
Suburban	1
Small City/Town	1
Rural	0
Total:	**3**

Security Devices Maintained By Victim Institutions

Alarm System	3
Surveillance Cameras	3
Bait Money	1
Guards	0
Currency Dye/Gas Packs	1
Electronic Tracking Devices	0
Bullet-Resistant Enclosures	0

Security Devices Used During Crimes

Alarm System Activated	1
Surveillance Cameras Activated	1
Bait Money Taken	0
Guards on Duty	0
Currency Dye/Gas Packs Taken	0
Electronic Tracking Devices Activated	0

Modus Operandi Used

Demand note Used	1
Firearm Used	0
Other Weapon Used	0
Weapon Threatened	0
Explosive Device Used or Threatened	1
Telephone Call	0

Injuries, Deaths, and Hostages Taken

There were no injuries, deaths, or hostages taken during this time frame.

III. BANK ROBBERY STATUE VIOLATIONS BY REGIONS, GEOGRAPHIC DIVISION, STATES, AND TERRITORIES
January 1, 2016 - December 31, 2016

	BANK ROBBERIES	BANK BURGLARIES	BANK LARCENIES	BANK EXTORTIONS
REGIONAL SUMMARY				
NORTHEAST	1,022	20	1	0
NORTH CENTRAL	849	9	0	1
SOUTH	1,292	18	0	1
WEST	1,013	18	0	1
TERRITORIES	9	0	0	0
TOTALS:	**4,185**	**65**	**1**	**3**
NORTHEAST	**1,022**	**20**	**1**	**0**
NEW ENGLAND	315	3	1	0
CONNECTICUT	72	0	0	0
MAINE	0	0	0	0
MASSACHUSETTS	243	3	1	0
NEW HAMPSHIRE	0	0	0	0
RHODE ISLAND	0	0	0	0
VERMONT	0	0	0	0
MIDDLE ATLANTIC	707	17	0	0
NEW JERSEY	100	2	0	0
NEW YORK	371	14	0	0
PENNSYLVANIA	236	1	0	0
NORTH CENTRAL	**849**	**9**	**0**	**1**
EAST NORTH CENTRAL	650	4	0	0
ILLINOIS	215	0	0	0
INDIANA	88	0	0	0
MICHIGAN	98	3	0	0
OHIO	171	1	0	0
WISCONSIN	78	0	0	0
WEST NORTH CENTRAL	199	5	0	1
IOWA	0	0	0	0
KANSAS	0	0	0	0
MINNESOTA	58	0	0	1
MISSOURI	66	1	0	0
NEBRASKA	75	4	0	0
NORTH DAKOTA	0	0	0	0
SOUTH DAKOTA	0	0	0	0

SOUTH	1,292	18	0	1
SOUTH ATLANTIC	756	4	0	1
DELAWARE	0	0	0	0
DISTRICT OF COLUMBIA	53	0	0	0
FLORIDA	213	1	0	1
GEORDIA	103	0	0	0
MARYLAND	159	1	0	0
NORTH CAROLINA	107	0	0	0
SOUTH CAROLINA	38	2	0	0
VIRGINIA	83	0	0	0
WEST VIRGINIA	0	0	0	0
EAST SOUTH CENTRAL	139	2	0	0
ALABAMA	32	1	0	0
KENTUCKY	41	1	0	0
MISSISSIPPI	15	0	0	0
TENNESSEE	51	0	0	0
WEST SOUTH CENTRAL	397	12	0	0
ARKANSAS	25	2	0	0
LOUISIANA	34	4	0	0
OKLAHOMA	37	1	0	0
TEXAS	301	5	0	0
WEST	1,013	18	0	1
MOUNTAIN	337	3	0	1
ARIZONA	106	1	0	0
COLORADO	113	2	0	1
IDAHO	0	0	0	0
MONTANA	0	0	0	0
NEVADA	48	0	0	0
NEW MEXICO	1	0	0	0
UTAH	69	0	0	0
WYOMING	0	0	0	0
PACIFIC	676	15	0	0
ALASKA	10	1	0	0
CALIFORNIA	462	12	0	0
HAWAII	15	1	0	0
OREGON	41	1	0	0
WASHINGTON	148	0	0	0
TERRITORIES	9	0	0	0
GUAM	0	0	0	0
PUETO RICO	9	0	0	0
VIRGIN ISLANDS	0	0	0	0
TOTALS:	4,185	65	1	3

IV. VIOLATIONS INVOLVING ARMORED CARRIERS INVESTIGATED UNDER THE HOBBS ACT
TITLE 18, UNITED STATES CODE,
SECTION 1951
January 1, 2016 - December 31, 2016

Armored Carrier Violations

Hobbs Act	36
TOTAL:	**36**

Number, Race, and Sex of Perpetrators

The number of persons known to be involved in the 36 armored carrier violations was 63. In a number of cases the number and description of individuals involved is unknown due to nonobservance of the perpetrators by the victim(s) or the use of disguises. The following table shows a breakdown of the 63 known individuals involved by race and sex:

	White	Black	Hispanic	Asian	Other	Unknown
Male	2	35	11	0	0	15
Female	0	0	0	0	0	0

Unknown Race/Sex: 0

Occurrences by Day of Week and Time of Day

Monday	-	7	6-9 a.m.	-	7
Tuesday	-	8	9-11 a.m.	-	6
Wednesday	-	2	11 a.m.-1 p.m.	-	7
Thursday	-	2	1-3 p.m.	-	6
Friday	-	7	3-6 p.m.	-	7
Saturday	-	9	6 p.m.-6 a.m.	-	3
Sunday	-	1	Not Determined	-	0
Not Determined	-	0			
Total:		**36**	**Total:**		**36**

Institution Community Characteristics

Facility Location

Commercial District	16
Shopping Center	15
Residential	4
Other Location	1
Total:	**36**

Community Type

Metropolitan	26
Suburban	7
Small City/Town	2
Rural	1
Total:	**36**

Modus Operandi Used

Firearm Used	22
Handgun[4]	34
Other Firearm	7
Other Weapon Used[5]	2
Weapon Threatened[6]	10
Explosive Device Used or Threatened	0
Oral Demand	7
Vault or Safe Theft	0

Injuries, Deaths, and Hostages Taken

Acts of violence were committed during 20 of the 36 armored carrier violations that occurred during this time frame. These acts included 13 instances involving the discharge of firearms, seven instances involving assaults, and no hostages were taken when the violent acts were committed. These acts of violence resulted in 14 injuries and three deaths. (One or more acts of violence may occur during an incident.)

Injuries

Customer	1
Employee	1
Employee Family	0
Perpetrator	4
Law Officer	1
Guard	7
Other	0
Total:	**14**

Number of violations in which injuries occurred: 11

Deaths

Customer	0
Employee	0
Employee Family	0
Perpetrator	1
Law Officer	0
Guard	2
Other	0
Total:	**3**

Number of violations in which deaths occurred: 3

---

[4] 'Handgun' and 'Other Firearm' added together may not coincide with 'Firearm Used' since, in some cases, both handguns and other firearms are used in the same crime.

[5] 'Other Weapon Used' includes knives, other cutting instruments, clubs, etc.

[6] 'Weapon Threatened' includes those cases where a weapon was threatened or implied either orally or in a demand note but not actually observed or displayed.

Any statistical information furnished in this booklet is subject to change upon the investigation of bank robbery violations which occurred during 2016.

The BCS provides a nationwide view of bank robbery crimes based on statistics contributed by FBI field offices responding to bank robberies or otherwise gathered when provided to the FBI from local and state law enforcement.

Statistics recorded as of 5/17/2017, at FBI Headquarters.

NOTE: Not all bank robberies are reported to the FBI, and therefore BCS is not a complete statistical compilation of all bank robberies that occur in the United States.

Printed in Great Britain
by Amazon

21862807R00020